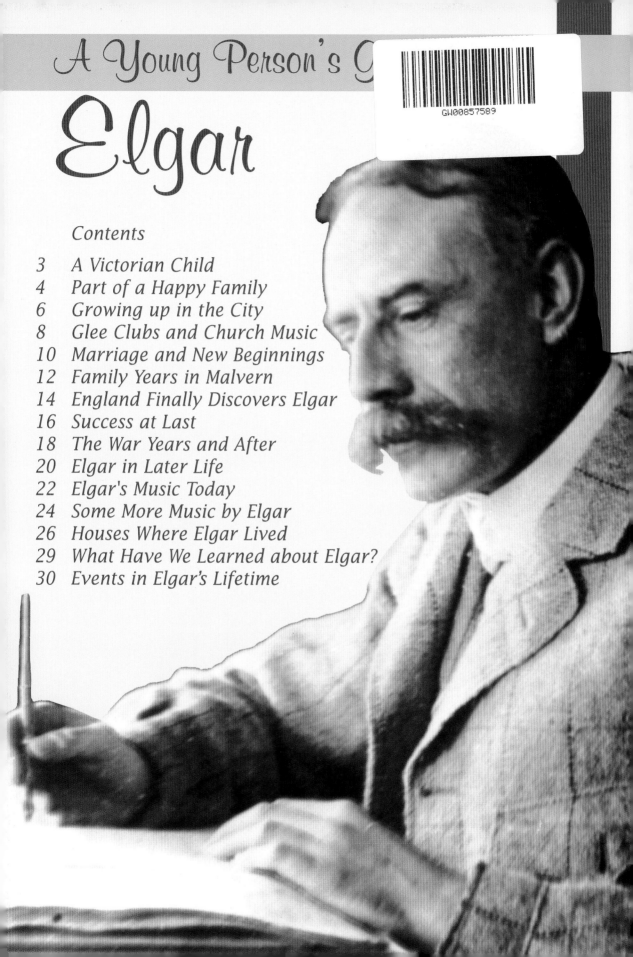

A Young Person's G...

Elgar

Contents

Published in Great Britain by

Elgar Editions

for

Elgar Foundation Enterprises Ltd
The Elgar Birthplace Museum, Crown East Lane, Lower Broadheath, Worcester WR2 6RH

© Elgar Foundation Enterprises Ltd, 2005

First Published: July 2005

British Library Cataloguing in Publication Data
A Catalogue record for this book is available from the British Library

ISBN 0 9548553 2 9 (Elgar Editions)

Acknowledgements:

Chris Bennett, John Norris, Elizabeth Pimblett, Cathy Sloan, Ann Vernau, David Birtwhistle

Printed and bound in Great Britain by
Pershore Print
49 High Street, Pershore
Worcestershire WR10 1EU

In this picture of Elgar aged about two with his mother Ann, the young boy wears a dress. Victorian boys did not wear breeches [trousers] until they were older.

Edward William Elgar was born in 1857, when Queen Victoria had been queen of England and the British Empire for 20 years. He was born at Newbury Cottage in the village of Lower Broadheath in Worcestershire. His mother was a farmer's daughter and a writer of poetry, and it was her wish that the family home should be in the countryside.

When Edward was two or three, the Elgar family moved back into Worcester city, but the children came back to Broad-heath for holidays, and the place was always special to Elgar.

In this sketch by a family friend, Harry, Susannah and Lucy are in the garden. Jack the pony is in the stable that Elgar's father and uncle built.

3

Edward Elgar with his brother Frank, sisters Lucy, Susannah and Helen, and their pet dog.

Edward Elgar was one of seven children. He had an older brother Harry, three sisters called Lucy, Susannah (Pollie) and Helen (Dot), and two younger brothers, Frank and Frederick (Joe). It was a happy family, with a love of pets. Although they were not rich, they had a maid called Maria, and the older children spent their time bowling hoops, making music, keeping hens and creating a secret imaginary world filled with fairies, giants, bears, moths and other creatures.

Part of a Happy Family

© David Birtwhistle

When he was an old man, Elgar still remembered his childhood fondly. Here he is seen feeding chickens, just as he and his brothers and sisters did many years earlier.

All the boys were good at music from a young age. (We do not know if the sisters studied an instrument, but they did sing in the choir.) Sadly both Harry and Joe died, one from scarlet fever and the other from tuberculosis. Today these illnesses can be cured, but in Victorian times many families lost a child.

5

When the Elgar family moved back into Worcester city, they lived in the rooms above the family's music shop near the cathedral.

BY APPOINTMENT TO HER LATE MAJESTY QUEEN ADELAIDE.

ELGAR BROTHERS,
FOREIGN AND ENGLISH
Pianoforte and Music Warehouse.
CONCERT, GRAND, OBLIQUE, & COTTAGE PIANOFORTES,
By Broadwood, Collard, Erard, Kirkman, and other London Makers,
From 25 to 150 Guineas, for Sale or Hire.
Drawing-room, Model, and Church Harmoniums,
From 6 to 70 Guineas.
AGENTS FOR RAMSDEN'S MELODY HARMONIUMS.
New Music at Half-price.   Instruments Let on Hire, with option of Purchase, on most
advantageous terms.   Pianofortes Tuned, Repaired, or taken in Exchange.
CONCERT AGENTS.

10, HIGH STREET, WORCESTER.

This publication has been produced by The Elgar Society. Details of the Society and application form for membership may be obtained by writing to the Secretary,
17 Earlsfield Road, Wandsworth Comm
ISBN 0 95

Edward Elgar's father, William Elgar, was a piano tuner. He went to the big country houses, making sure that their pianos sounded just right, and worked for the widowed Queen Adelaide when she lived at Witley Court in Worcestershire. As a boy, Edward would sometimes go with him. They would have to use the "tradesmen's entrance" to these grand houses, not the front door like important visitors did.

Elgar's parents

Growing up in the City

Elgar attended school until the age of 15, which was a couple of years more than most children at this time. Although he had violin and piano lessons, for someone wanting to become a composer, he would have been expected to study at a university as well. Elgar however taught himself all about music. In his father's shop he found books of music by composers like Beethoven, and took these on his walks in the countryside to study them.

Right: Elgar, aged 14.

Below: Worcester High Street, seen here in 1904. The Elgar Brothers music shop is on the left.

Mr. Edward Elgar,

Violinist,

(Pupil of Herr A. Pollitzer, London),

βEGS to announce that he visits Malvern
and neighbourhood to give Violin Lessons,
advanced and elementary. Also Lessons in
Accompaniment and Ensemble playing.

For Terms, &c., address 4, Field Terrace,
Worcester.

*Elgar's advert
offering to give violin lessons.*

The Elgar boys and their father played in music clubs in and around Worcester, and William Elgar was paid to play the organ at St. George's Catholic Church. Edward was brought up a Catholic by his mother. In Victorian England, most people belonged to the Anglican church, and many of them looked down on Catholics. Elgar was very aware of this. However he loved the music that was performed in the great Anglican Cathedral. So much so that, as soon as the service at St George's had finished, he would rush down the High Street to hear it.

STRUGGLING TO EARN MONEY THROUGH MUSIC

When he left school Edward was sent to work in a law office but didn't like it and soon left. Over the next few years he earned money teaching the violin and piano, and conducting a dance band at the Powick Lunatic Asylum. Sometimes he was paid to write short pieces of dance music. He was quite poor. These were very difficult years, but they taught him a lot about how to write music for all the different instruments of the orchestra. During this time he left home to live with a married sister Pollie.

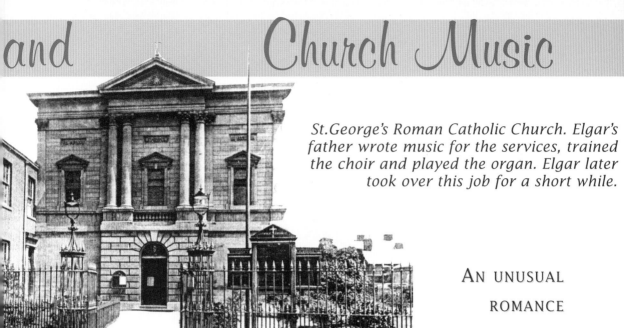

St. George's Roman Catholic Church. Elgar's father wrote music for the services, trained the choir and played the organ. Elgar later took over this job for a short while.

An unusual romance

In 1886, Edward Elgar started to teach piano in Malvern to a lady who came from Gloucestershire, Caroline Alice Roberts (known as Alice). Alice's father had been a Major-General in the Army. She had written a novel called *Marchcroft Manor* and some poetry, and lived at home with her widowed mother.

Powick Asylum, where Elgar once conducted the staff band. The building has since been knocked down.

Marriage

To the Victorians, Miss Roberts' family was far above Elgar's, who were "in trade" and worked for a living. But Alice and Edward fell in love. When they became engaged, Elgar wrote a piece of music for her, *Salut d'amour*.

Her family disapproved of her engagement. Bravely, Alice became a Catholic and in 1889 married Elgar at

Mr. and Mrs. Elgar on holiday in Germany in 1897.

Brompton Oratory in London, where they set up home. Alice was forty, several years older than her husband.

"I must tell you how happy I am in my new life & what a dear, loving companion I have & how sweet everything seems..." Edward Elgar 6th October 1889.

Somehow Alice knew that her husband was a genius, and during their marriage Elgar wrote his most famous works. Alice still wrote poems and some of these Elgar set to music.

HARD TIMES

Elgar was working very hard to get his music known, but England did not seem very interested. The Elgars lived in London for only two years. Elgar advertised for pupils in the city as a music teacher, but he had no replies. During this time Elgar was inspired to write his first important piece of music, the overture *Froissart*, which was played at the Worcester Three Choirs Festival. Because of their lack of money, Alice had to sell some of her jewellery to keep the family going, and they were forced to come back to Malvern where Elgar was better known.

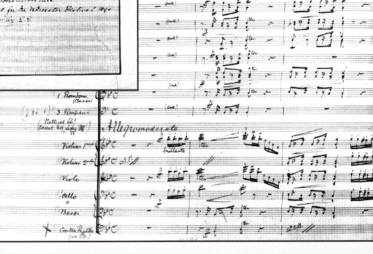

The title page of Froissart. Elgar would often add cartoons and quotations to his scores ...

... and a page from the manuscript score. Alice would draw the lines of the staves in pen and ink to save money.

Family Years

Their only child, a daughter Carice, was born in London in 1890. Elgar invented her name by joining the names Caroline and Alice together. (He liked playing with words, puzzles and crosswords.) Later, Carice was sent to boarding school in Malvern, but used to fly kites and do scientific experiments with her father in the holidays.

*Carice aged about ten.
Her headmistress described her as being
a beautiful but very solemn child.*

Elgar in the laboratory he built to try out chemistry experiments.

in Malvern

Elgar taught the violin at local schools, and hated it, but it brought in money. Sometimes he would turn up to teach still dressed in his tweed golfing clothes, which shocked some people.

Elgar had many other interests apart from golf, and he loved the new sport of bicycling. He went for miles around the country lanes, and said that some of his musical ideas came to him when he was cycling.

In the 1890s the Elgars went on several holidays to Germany, and really enjoyed it. Elgar wrote the music *From The Bavarian Highlands* for which Alice wrote the words.

'Nimrod' (August Jaeger), the most famous of the Variations.

During the next few years, Elgar wrote several important works, each more ambitious than the last. He was becoming quite well known as a composer and he was now often asked to write pieces for important festivals in the Midlands and North of England.

But the work that really made Elgar famous, and one that many people remember him for today, is the *Enigma Variations* (1898-99). The music was an instant success with critics, who saw it as something new and exciting. In it, Elgar paints musical pictures of a number of his and Alice's friends by, for example, arranging the main tune in the way the friend might have played it. One Variation is meant to show a friend's bulldog, Dan (right), falling into the river, swimming to the bank, climbing out and barking.

Elgar also hinted that the music contained a hidden theme but, even today, nobody has been able to discover what it is.

Birchwood Lodge, the country cottage in which Elgar wrote The Dream of Gerontius. *...dward and Alice Elgar can be seen standing outside.*

In 1900 Elgar was invited to write a major work for the Birmingham Festival. He finished the work in a country cottage he rented; it was a setting for voices of a famous poem *The Dream of Gerontius* written by the Catholic priest Cardinal Newman. At the Festival the choir had not practiced it enough and the performance did not go well. But the next performance in Dusseldorf, Germany in 1901 was much better.

Cockaigne, a musical picture of London, was however, a great success, and in 1901, Elgar wrote his first *Pomp and Circumstance March*. When it was first played, the audience loved it so much that it had to be played three times in a row.

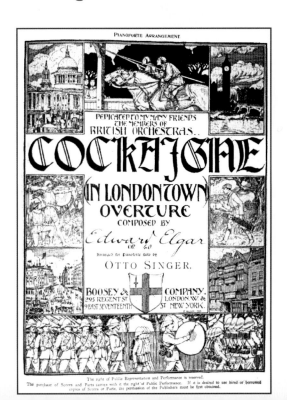

Left: Elgar wearing his Court Dress with his Order of Merit medal which he received in 1911.

Right: a cartoon of Elgar conducting, drawn by Ernest Forbes in 1900.

Over the next few years Elgar's star continued to rise. He wrote more and more important works, including two symphonies, and concertos for violin and cello, and he mixed with the most important people in society at the time. He had come a long way from the "Worcester tradesman's son" but he always stayed true to Worcestershire and his friends. In 1904 he was knighted and became "Sir Edward Elgar", and he made sure he told his widowed father first.

In 1905 Elgar was given the honour of Freedom of the City of Worcester, and in 1911 he received the Order of Merit from the King, an honour given to very few people.

Elgar leaving the Guildhall in Worcester after being given the Freedom of the City.

Elgar started to conduct his music for the gramophone companies. Recording technology was very new and exciting - now people could listen to whole orchestras in their own house! Elgar thought that it was marvellous.

Right: Elgar poses for an advert for an HMV gramophone while, below, he conducts a recording of Carissima.

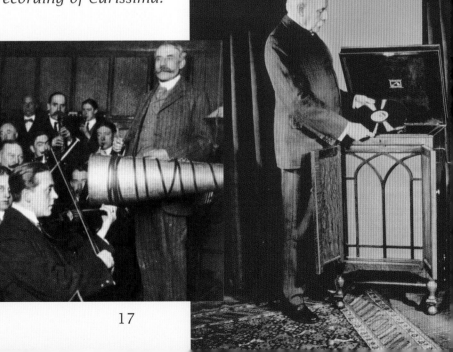

Alice Elgar at Severn House, their home in Hampstead.

In 1912, the Elgars moved again to London, settling in Hampstead. Two years later, when they were on holiday in Scotland, the Great War broke out. This has become known as the First World War, and suddenly the Germany that the Elgars had loved, and which had loved his music, was now Britain's enemy. Elgar was too old to be a soldier abroad. He wrote some music to help war charities in Belgium and Poland, but became unhappy and unable to work until he retreated to a cottage called 'Brinkwells' in the Sussex countryside. Here he composed three pieces of chamber music now recognised as being among his greatest works.

Brinkwells, their cottage in Sussex.

... and After

The grave of Sir Edward and Lady Elgar in St Wulstan's churchyard, Little Malvern.

THE END OF A SPECIAL MARRIAGE

The war had ended in 1918, but for Elgar the sadness was not to stop. In 1919 in London, Alice was as usual helping Elgar edit his music, but was becoming increasingly unwell. In April 1920 she died. Elgar said :

"All I have done was owing to her and I am at present a sad and broken man - just stunned."

She was buried at Little Malvern.

Elgar felt lonely after Alice died, and spent much time with Carice and friends. He sold 'Severn House' and returned to Worcestershire, where he would take car rides round the lanes he had always loved.

An advert for the house Elgar sold when he moved away from London.

Above: Elgar and Marco in the garden of 'Marl Bank', Elgar's last house.

Below: The brochure from the trip Elgar took after Alice's death.

1,000 Miles up the Amazon

Right: Elgar with the playwright George Bernard Shaw.

Far right: Elgar about to board the flight to France.

Alice did not like dogs but, after he returned to Worcestershire, Elgar was able to keep them as pets once more. They adored him and he would let them sit on chairs at the dinner table.

He also took a trip up the River Amazon in South America, made a close friend in the writer George Bernard Shaw, and in 1933 quite daringly flew in an early passenger aeroplane to France to visit the violinist Yehudi Menuhin and the composer Delius.

Elgar found it difficult to write music after Alice's death, although he kept conducting. He eventually wrote short pieces, such as the *Civic Fanfare* for Hereford Three Choirs Festival, and the *Nursery Suite* in 1931 for the Duke and Duchess of York and princesses Elizabeth and Margaret Rose. Elizabeth would later become queen.

His friends wanted to encourage him to write serious music once more, and in 1932 he was asked by the BBC to write a new symphony, his third. It was starting to come together from little sketches when Elgar had to have an operation on his stomach. The news was not good, and Elgar was never to finish his last, great work. He died

Elgar working on his Third Symphony.

at Worcester in 1934 and is buried next to Alice at Little Malvern. So Elgar is still in the area that he loved so much.

One of the last honours that Elgar received was to be made a Baronet, and he chose to be called Sir Edward Elgar of Broadheath, where he had been born.

The Royal Albert Hall, London, where Elgar's music is played each year at Proms concerts.

Today much of Elgar's music is played regularly in Britain at concerts and on the radio and television. The pieces listed in the box below are well-liked and well-known, and are also often used as theme tunes and background music for programmes and adverts. Do you know any of them?

SOME WELL-KNOWN WORKS BY ELGAR
- ☐ *Enigma Variations* (especially 'Nimrod')
- ☐ *Land of Hope and Glory*
- ☐ *The Dream of Gerontius*
- ☐ *'Cello Concerto*
- ☐ the symphonies
- ☐ *Salut d'Amour*
- ☐ *Chanson de Matin*

AND SOME LESS WELL-KNOWN WORKS
- ☐ *Dream Children*
- ☐ *The Wand of Youth* Suites
- ☐ *Nursery Suite*

Elgar's music is also played in several other countries, especially America and Japan, but quite a few countries have not yet really discovered Elgar. And even in Britain, there are a number of works by Elgar that should be played much more often than they are.

Music Today

King Edward VII.

LAND OF HOPE AND GLORY

In 1901, Elgar had composed his first *Pomp and Circumstance March*. This had been a great success and the Prince of Wales, soon to become King Edward VII, had told Elgar how much he liked it. When Queen Victoria died (also in 1901), Elgar was asked to compose some special music for the crowning ceremony of the new King Edward and Queen Alexandra. Elgar asked the writer A.C. Benson to put words to the March that the King had liked, and this new piece became what we know today as *Land of Hope and Glory*.

SALUT D'AMOUR

Just before he became engaged to Alice, Elgar went on holiday to Yorkshire with an old friend, Dr. Charles Buck. As he was leaving Worcester, Alice gave Elgar a poem she had written called *Love's Grace* so, while in Yorkshire, Elgar composed a short piece of music for her called *Love's Greeting*. He managed to sell the piece to a music publisher who decided a French title would make the music more popular, and the piece became *Salut d'Amour*, the name we all know it by.

Elgar and Yehudi Menuhin.

THE VIOLIN CONCERTO

In 1910, Elgar completed a *Violin Concerto*, a work in which a solo violinist is accompanied by an orchestra. On the title page, Elgar wrote "Here is enshrined the soul of .....". Like the *Enigma Variations*, many people have since tried to discover the person Elgar was thinking of. In 1932, less than two years before he died, Elgar made a very famous recording of this work with a young violinist called Yehudi Menuhin. You can still find this recording in CD shops today.

WAND OF YOUTH

When musical ideas came to him, Elgar would jot these down in scrap books. Even at the height of his fame, he retained fond memories of his childhood and looked back into his scrapbooks to put together two collections of tunes he had used for the plays he had performed as a young boy with his brothers and sisters. He called these his *Wand of Youth Suites*. The names of the tunes show their childhood origins: 'Fairies and Giants'; 'Moths and Butterflies'; 'The Little Bells'; 'Fountain Dance'; 'The Tame Bear' and 'Wild Bears'.

Music by Elgar

CARACTACUS – A LOCAL MASTERPIECE

In 1897 Elgar's mother Ann pointed to the grand hillfort called British Camp that is part of the Malvern Hills, and asked Edward if something could be written about it. Elgar wrote the cantata *Caractacus*, based on the life of a Celtic king who fought against the Roman invasion. When Elgar was seriously ill in later life, it was the 'Woodland Interlude' from this local work that he wished to hear.

NURSERY SUITE

In 1931, by now an old man, Elgar returned once more to his scrapbooks to put together a third collection of short tunes which he called the *Nursery Suite*. He dedicated this suite to the Duke and Duchess of York and the Princesses Elizabeth (who later became Queen Elizabeth II) and Margaret Rose. Later in the same year, he conducted a recording of the *Nursery Suite*. In those days, recordings were cut straight onto a record and editing was not possible. One piece was slightly too long to fit on one side of the record, so Elgar had to record it again, making the orchestra play it a little faster.

Houses Where Elgar Lived

Elgar lived in more than 20 houses during his lifetime. Some of them for no more than a few months, others for several years, and after he became famous the houses he chose were quite grand. Apart from the Elgar Birthplace Museum, all of the remaining houses are still used as private homes.

CRAEG LEA, MALVERN WELLS. This house stands beside the main road from Malvern to Malvern Wells. Elgar made up the name from the letters ELGAR and the initial letters of Edward, Alice and Carice. There is a plaque on the gatepost with a picture of Elgar's head on it. He lived here from 1899 until 1904, the years during which he and his music became famous throughout England. He loved the view from the front of the house across the valley of the River Severn and decided to move away when he heard of plans to build houses that he feared would spoil the view.

PLAS GWYN, HEREFORD. This is the house that the Elgars moved to from Craeg Lea. It is on the road from Hereford to Mordiford Bridge, where Elgar often went fishing. He built a laboratory in one of the outbuildings so that he could carry out chemical experiments as a hobby. He also composed some great music here, including the *Symphony No.1*, the *Violin Concerto* and *The Wand of Youth Suites*. Eventually, the need to live closer to London forced them to give up the house and move in 1912.

NAPLETON GRANGE, KEMPSEY. After the death of his wife, Elgar longed to return to his native Worcestershire and in 1923 he rented Napleton Grange, a large house set in the countryside outside the village of Kempsey, south of Worcester. He did not compose very much music during the four years he lived here and spent much of his time revisiting favourite places and watching horse-racing.

... and his Birthplace

The Birthplace Cottage, 3 miles west of Worcester, is signposted off the A44 Worcester/Leominster road.

THE ELGAR BIRTHPLACE, LOWER BROADHEATH. Of all the places in which he lived, Elgar always retained a particular fondness for the cottage in Broad-heath, a small village 3 miles west of Worcester, in which he was born. After his death, his daughter Carice managed to persuade the Council to buy the birthplace cottage so that it could be turned into a museum in memory of her father. If you visit the cottage today, you will find a large collection of objects connected with the composer's life, many of which belonged to Elgar himself, and in the adjacent Elgar Centre, you can learn more about his life and hear some of his music.

Above: The Elgar Centre.

Right: Looking from the Birthplace towards Birmingham.

What Have We Learnt ...

1. In which village was Elgar born?
2. For which two musical instruments did Elgar have lessons?
3. In which road did Severn House stand?
4. Who wrote the poem *The Dream of Gerontius*, which Elgar set to music?
5. In which of Elgar's works will you find the 'Fountain Dance'?
6. Where is Alice Elgar buried?
7. What did Elgar's father do for a living?
8. Where did Elgar often go fishing?
9. Who wrote the words for *Land of Hope and Glory*?
10. What was the name of the first important piece of music Elgar composed?
11. Who or what was Dan, pictured in the *Enigma Variations*?
12. By what nickname was Elgar's sister Susannah known?
13. Who commissioned Elgar to write his *Third Symphony*?
14. Which town or city is pictured in the *Cockaigne* Overture?
15. In which year was Elgar knighted?
16. When was Elgar's daughter Carice born?
17. What was the name of the cottage the Elgars rented in Sussex?
18. Where did Alice and Edward marry?
19. Who did Elgar visit during his trip to France in 1933?
20. For which two solo instruments did Elgar write concertos?

... about Elgar?

Answers: 1. Lower Broadheath; 2. violin; piano; 3. Netherhall Gardens; 4. Cardinal Newman; 5. *The Wand of Youth Suites*; 6. Little Malvern; 7. A piano tuner (and music shop keeper); 8. Mordiford Bridge; 9. A.C. Benson; 10. *Froissart Overture*; 11. A bulldog; 12. Pollie; 13. The BBC; 14. London; 15. 1904; 16. 1890; 17. Brinkwells; 18. Brompton Oratory, London; 19. Yehudi Menuhin; Frederick Delius the composer; 20. violin; cello

Queen Victoria

1837 Victoria becomes Queen

1848 Caroline Alice Roberts born

1857 Elgar born 2 June at Broadheath; Indian Mutiny

1875 First Gilbert and Sullivan opera performed

1876 Alexander Graham Bell invents the telephone

1877 Queen Victoria becomes Empress of India; Thomas Edison invents the phonograph, forerunner of the gramophone

1883 Death of composer Richard Wagner

1885 Elgar succeeds his father as organist of St George's RC Church, Worcester

Richard Wagner

Peter Ilyich Tchaikovsky

1888 Elgar composes *Salut d'Amour* for Alice; Eastman company produce first Kodak camera

1889 Elgar marries Caroline Alice Roberts on 8 May

1890 Elgar composes *Froissart Overture*, his first major orchestral work; daughter Carice born 14 August

1893 Death of composer Peter Ilyich Tchaikovsky

1895 The first season of Henry Wood Promenade Concerts

1896 Elgar composes *King Olaf*, his first concert-length choral work

1897 Death of composer Johannes Brahms

1898 First performance of *Caractacus*

1899 First performance of the *Enigma Variations*; the second Boer War begins

1900 First performance of *The Dream of Gerontius*; Elgar awarded Honorary Doctorate by Cambridge University

Johannes Brahms

1901 First performance of *Pomp and Circumstance Marches Nos.1 and 2*, and *Cockaigne Overture*; Queen Victoria dies

Elgar's Lifetime

1902 Second Boer War ends

1903 First performance of *The Apostles*

1904 Three day Elgar Festival at Covent Garden; Elgar knighted

Covent Garden Opera House in 1904

1905 First performance of *Introduction and Allegro for Strings*

1907 Elgar composes *Wand of Youth Suite No.1*

1908 First performance of *Symphony No.1* and *Wand of Youth* Suite No.2; Robert Baden-Powell founds Boy Scout movement

1910 First performance of Elgar's *Violin Concerto*

1911 First performance of Elgar's *Symphony No.2*; Elgar becomes a member of the Order of Merit

1912 Elgar moves to London; *Titanic* sinks

1914 Elgar conducts his first gramophone recording *Carissima*; First World War begins

Elgar's OM medal

1918 First World War ends

1918-9 Elgar composes chamber works and the *'Cello Concerto*

1919 First non-stop trans-atlantic flight by Alcock and Brown

1920 Lady Elgar dies 7 April; radio broadcasting begins

1923 Elgar returns to Worcestershire, visits South America for a cruise up the Amazon; first Wembley cup final

1924 Elgar appointed Master of the King's Musick

1926 John Logie Baird demonstrates television

1928 Walt Disney introduces Mickey Mouse

1931 Elgar composes the *Nursery Suite*, and opens EMI recording studio at Abbey Road, London

Plaque at Abbey Road studios.

1932 Elgar conducts Yehudi Menuhin in a recording of the *Violin Concerto*

1934 Elgar dies peacefully on 23 February in Worcester

1935 Birthplace Cottage purchased by Worcester City Council

When Elgar was 64 years old, he wrote to his good friend Sidney Colvin:

"I am still at heart the dreamy child who used to be found in the reeds by Severn side with a sheet of paper, trying to fix the sounds and longing for something very great. I am still looking for This ..."